To NYC
An Ongoing and Rough Ode to my Place of Birth
William George Cockrell

Plum Publishing Co. Ltd.

Copyright © 2025 by William G. Cockrell and Plum Publishing Co. Ltd.

Published by Plum Publishing Co. Ltd.

Pitkin County, Colorado

First Edition

ISBN: 979-8-9883801-5-3

All rights reserved.

No portion of this book may be reproduced in any form without written permission from the publisher or author, except as permitted by U.S. copyright law.

Contents

Introduction	IV
Note by the Author	VI
I.	1
II.	2
III.	3
IV.	5
In Memory of the Author	6

Introduction
By Tucker D. Farris

The poem contained in this book is an unfinished ode to New York City written by my dear childhood friend William G. Cockrell in January of 2021. He sent it to me in this state accompanied by the note following this introduction while I spent the winter holiday away from Victoria, British Columbia in his adoptive and my own childhood hometown of Carbondale, Colorado. The ode he composed was one that to my knowledge he had never finished before his death, and it was one that he had seemingly not shared with anyone else at the time of composition.

It is a short piece, composed of only nineteen stanzas and ordered into four parts. The first is untitled, and parts II-IV contain titled fragments that presuppose the collected stanzas. I am unsure if they were intentional buffers for separate sections or lines in their own rite. I have opted here, in his memory to assume the former.

I have wrestled with the possession of this work by my late friend for what will be three years come August. I have shared it with his family, and have had the intent to publish it posthumously in his name for almost the entire time between tucking my personal annotated copy of *Nausea* by Jean-Paul Sartre in his hands prior to his cremation. I have grappled with the vision of publication for the entirety of this time. Initially, I had planned to compose 19 corresponding colour illustrations to accompany each stanza myself. I completed a handful of these using charcoal, pencil and some very strange acrylic paint pens, but as I look back upon them, I feel there is too much of my grief and interpretation of my friend Will in them for wide-scale publication. They are more reflective of my experience of his poem than they are of the words, and so I fear that by continuing to compose them, I would be unfairly asserting an aesthetic that did not belong to his words.

And so I decided that the first edition of his work *To NYC* would be released into the world in the purest form of the written word. Without illustrations, and without decoration. Chic minimalism I would quip to him if instead of the caretaker of his posthumous publication, I were his living editor. At some point in the future, I envision a limited run of illustrated copies, but for now, his words I think must shine in the black and white of the page.

To my knowledge, this is one of the very rare few piece of Will's writings that survive today aside from his master's thesis. It is certainly the only poetry of Will's that I know to exist.

I have not edited this work beyond typesetting, and the only other inclusion in this text, in lieu of an 'about the author' section is a long form obituary I composed at Will's passing to immortalize our experiences together in memoriam.

I am therefore proud to present this here for the reader free of my interpretive lens, and free of claims to speak for the author in his absence.

What I will offer only in passing is that my reading of the poem for the first time, as well as each subsequent time has been an emotionally visceral experience. Will was quite adept at conjuring a visual viscera in his speech and in this poem. It evokes a moderate discomfort at times, and a raw power throughout. There is a darkness to it, something that I believe partially romanticizes his hometown and childhood in New York in synthesis with a broader 1970s aesthetic of the place. He melds history, subversion, deviance, crime, debauchery and horror into something that feels entirely disconnected while somehow still concisely present as if it were a recounting of the reader's own memories. It is special both in its compositional style, but also in its intimacy. It is something that a prolific thinker *chose* to write, and it was therefore somewhere quite close to his creative heart.

Should his spirit find this text somewhere, I do hope that in his wry sense of humour he does not warmly chastise me too strongly for my presumptuous pretentiousness in publishing his work.

And finally, I must offer the following:

In Loving Memory of William George Cockrell, Philosopher, Friend, Colleague, Brother, Son, and Good Man

Note by the Author

This is my ongoing and rough ode to my place of birth. I'd really like to know your opinion. Puns and entendres abound...

-William Cockrell,

January 19, 2021

568 Days Before his Death

I.

Pistol-whipped pimps sit like simple-headed simps with bracelets behind their backs on old New York curbs while we were smoking reefer in the depths of the park watching the metronome of French-Canadian mimes promising eternal youth in the light of Peter Pan in Yorkville

Saturday night disco shakers and breakers accompanied by prolific police brutality that batters the heartbeat of brave beasts and bareback sex, wrapping up investigations, cocks, cold cases, and the last call at the bar.

The world's Ellis Island where the best came in their younger and more formidable years carried away from the ebbs and tides of the Old World to settle anew in a paradise of their crude and cleve design, made by hand and born in an alchemy of blood and sweat.

II.

Only Here:

Blurbs blast across comics and pulp fiction paperbacks soaked with acid Reagan rain reigning regimented over ridiculous riddles of a rip-off Yellow Book mystic laying predatory in the text as if a call to her would execute a voodoo hex upon your enemies.

Vicarious violence affixed to voided checks, crack cooked in the depths of Hell's Kitchen ready for the man to ruck it to 125th where fiends and monsters conspire together as one to catch that next flight alone for a fiver

Subway lines pump pitiful pompous people proudly passing particles of pneumonia like pneumatic pressurized machinations of infinite ventricles of love and hate, and other emotions too

The city used to rattle rickety like a sleuthing snake sliding across the labia of oiled pros making ends to buy depends for kids raised by their grandmother in the West Village but especially the babushka who washed ashore widowed in Little Odessa still haunted by the Lienz Cossacks who were handed over to Stalin

III.
At the Only Spot:

Where Brother Malcolm straightened his hair before doing his concurrent bid, finding a lost prophet among perilous black destitution who bought him a star next to Jupiter and an avenue in Harlem for the price of buckshot

Where ad men contorted young minds to the will of cigarettes, booze, and fast cars bringing death and destruction back home in the prefrontal cortex before analysts had time to arrest dreadful sensations of guilts and confessions better suited for a young girl clasping her hands leaning her elbows looking up before she crawls into her bed

Where CIA funneled darkmoney expressed the abstract and aghast against Soviet incursions into the sensitive psyches of simple American sentiments overcoming the Gothic, honest work and dirt roads in exchange for stockbrokers, Walkmans and jogging around the reservoir

Where GIs and Marines who burned hooches out of spite, fear, and hate kicked dope while growing their hair out and keeping their moustaches stained with the yellow of softpack Marlboro combustion recalling stories of hoo-rahs at Khe-Sanh, Puking Buzzards at Hill 937 and the victories there

Where fanatics and fakes gathered around imagining how phony life will be while holding a cough in fields of strawberries behind a real sadness and depth that few probably knew, or wanted to

Where up north Bob Dylan committed sedition against the nation with electricity and cables, seemingly having surrendered to Edison as if he would turn the entire world into Menlo Park

IV.

In the place where:

Inside the Met is an Egyptian temple where curious imposters gather for fulfillment and wonder.

The stoic gaze of Nefertiti is not disturbed though she cries soundlessly weeping through the rape as to not to attract more attention.

Culture so visceral and vicious lays before lucky Caligulan Columbia grads racing through time with Benzedrine and the last lid of Acapulco Gold tucked inside the pocket of a twenty-two-year old's tweed jacket

Flaming Prometheans foraging Fire Island fetching the supreme moment of incandescent joy beyond repair before flumping back into perfumed French-stitched chairs fuming in their Wall Street corner offices, condensation on the windows

The statue of Liberty stands as a big middle-finger to all the dictators and tyrants who like the redcoat officer had his mouth bammed with the butt of a Brown Bess in Battery Park only to spit his teeth in south Hudson where the sewage now flows into the Atlantic

In Memory of the Author

August 12, 2022

Philosopher Thomas Nagel in an essay on the nature of death presents the notion that "Life is an episode between two oblivions." Wherein the limited space of time we come to occupy in our existence is one of grandeur and exigent beauty as a function of that limited nature of the space of our being. We occupy such a short time in the grand scheme of the universe such that our passing leaves imprinted upon those of us that remain among the living a heavy weight of loss and the notion of the negation of all future potential interactions. It is in these moments of loss that us remaining upon the living side of the veil of death are forced and encouraged to experience the life of the departed in our remembrance of them. In a social sense, there is an immortality of interaction, a living and breathing element of sanctuary in the memories of those that have gone on. It is in our recollection, in our reverence, and in our reflection that we come to not only celebrate the moments in time that we so luckily shared with those that have gone on, but we find ourselves sustaining them living in memoriam within the infinitely bound elements of our self and identity. All of this to say that the symbolic and socially meaningful moments of interaction we have shared with the deceased remain living beyond their physical death, wherein a metaphysical imprint of them lives on in the grief of their loss and the love of their remembrance.

"If is The Middle Word in Life"

I met Will at the stark young age of six or seven as I began my first year at the Carbondale Community School. Within the folds of this strange little hippie school in a special time and a special place Will and I became fast friends even though he was three grade levels ahead of me and one of the 'older kids'. Some of my earliest memories of knowing Will come from the Fall of 2004 wherein the context of our school we had begun having daily philosophical and political discussions on the swing sets during lunch recess under the Colorado sun. I as a ten-year-old was immediately amazed at the depth of intellect of this wonderful soul, and the conversations we had in these halcyon days of the first "W" Bush term were some that I feel first began to root my interest in the world external to me and beyond the simple wonderings of the average 4th grader. I distinctly remember the day of the 2004 presidential election where in the starkness of the November winter he and I met at recess to discuss the 'crushing' news to us kids that John Kerry had conceded the election to the second Bush and ushered in another four years. Looking back now in light of his passing, I might see how this was both deeply absurd in terms of the dramatic taking we had to Kerry's loss, but also that it was quite odd in the grander scheme of life that such young kids had already developed the intellectual capacity to recognize the geopolitical implications of such a historical moment (however insignificant it remains today).

That year we shared a scene group together in our school's all-school production known as "The Big Event" our scene was directed by Ted Frisbie, a teacher we had both come to love dearly. The scene was a humorous take on the ancient Greek Oracle of Delphi wherein various characters of Greek mythology visit a Peanuts style life coach kiosk that was originally managed by the oracle, but that had been taken over by the protagonists of the play. Will played the character of Icarus, the boy who while trapped with his father on the inescapable island of Crete fashioned together out of wax and feathers two pairs of wings they used to fly from the island. Icarus in the myth, flew too close to the Mediterranean sun and the wax of his wings melted causing him to fall to earth from the heavens. In our production, Will played a post-fall Icarus demanding aviation advice from the oracle who (unbeknownst to Icarus) had been replaced by time travelling kids suggest he just drink a Red Bull because "Red Bull Gives You Wings". Will delivered the famous tagline to raucous applause from the audience. In the principal's office 'backstage' the two nights of the production, Will as the 'cool' older kid of the group occupied the chair behind the desk, shared snacks with us and watched a movie. On both nights he cracked the Red Bull and with his feet on the principal's desk would wax poetic about the struggles and social goings on in the lives of us primary school kids. He embodied the bespoke and ever-elusive 'cool' identity even then.

The next year, Will and I again appeared in a scene in that year's production wherein the focal theme was art. Our scene explored the pop art movement and Will played the role of an amazing Andy Warhol. That spring during pre-production he and I shared several long afternoons spent out in the grass pouring over Warhol books and exploring the nature of pop art and the history of the rumbling counter culture of New York City. I knew then as I do now that Will would have instantly found home among the patrons of Warhol's Factory, where he would have jived with Lou Reed, John and Yoko and David Bowie without anyone ever questioning why he was there. Will was part outlaw philosopher, part beat poet, and part modern artist all in one. You could 'tell' with him that there was something transcendent. He had a Kerouac style to him, a Ginsberg insight, and the revolutionary bluster of Abbie Hoffman. Will was a once in a generation iconoclast that left an indelible impression upon me then in those formative years. There was something timeless about him where he could one moment embody Henry Kissinger in his political analysis and in the next talk about the upcoming James Bond movie (Die Another Day) all as we painted set backdrops to a loud stereo blasting American Idiot by Green Day.

This was how I came to know Will in the early days of his life. Before we stepped into the darkness of the real world that maturity brought with it. I am reminded now of a lyric by Shane MacGowan as I sit in reflection of these glory days of youth that encapsulates how I now had spent my time with Will as adults on Vancouver Island:

> *I've been loving you a long time*
> *Down all the years, down all the days*
> *And I've cried for all your troubles*
> *Smiled at your funny little ways*
> *We watched our friends grow up together*
> *And we saw them as they fell*
> *Some of them fell into Heaven*
> *Some of them fell into Hell*
> *I took shelter from a shower*
> *And I stepped into your arms*
> *On a rainy night in SoHo*
> *The wind was whistling all its charms*

The year of Warhol was Will's final year at the Community School. He graduated in the spring and went on to the inaccessible (to a 5th grader) world of high school. It is then when I lost connection with Will. I had little to no contact beyond the occasional Facebook birthday post. It is in these years that I later learn that Will met, danced with, and fought demons the likes of which would buckle any person less equipped with personal strength than he. For fifteen years or so I had not had the time nor pleasure of speaking with Will as life took us on our different paths. Him to Canada, me to follow in a more roundabout way. Somehow, in our time apart we found ourselves walking tangentially related paths in our academic work. Both becoming some kind of tangential outlaw philosopher in our own ways. Him at Queens in the realms of political theory and me in Victoria via Oregon in social philosophy. By chance two years ago Will moved to Victoria and we immediately rekindled that fiery relationship of sharp political and social discourse almost immediately.

Meeting for the first time in a decade and a half, Will and I shared a meal in the Faculty Club on campus and over the course of dinner and drinks we expounded upon both our shared history and that which had led us to this point in time together. It is in these moments that I found myself feeling the sense of comradeship that I had long since missed in the time between the Kerry/Bush election and then. There was an electricity to our discussions on the depths and boundless capacities of the human experience. Me in my existentialism, him in his political theory. We composed ideas, threw around co-authorships and melded together his love of Heidegger and min of Kierkegaard for endless chats over bottomless packs of cigarettes around the campus of The University of Victoria and beyond.

He came back into my life at a time of great personal upheaval for me as I struggled in a failing and abusive relationship. Will was and shall always be the one dear friend on Vancouver Island who not only listened to my endless problems, but offered not only support but firm and direct reflections on the darkness therein. In his ways, he shared with me his pain, his traumas, his horrors. And in our collective despair we found one another's souls as intellectual soulmates and the most endearing of platonic friends that anyone might experience. We called upon each other in moments of pure dark depravity on the lowest rung of our experiences as we tread water through the tumult of life itself. Will was no stranger to darkness, having fought his own battles with bravery, and emerging with the scars to prove that he survived victorious. Our talks were frank, bleak at times, and plumbed the depths of the capacity of the human spirit to experience the suffering of life.

However, in these depths we found ourselves providing a sense of lasting calm, of not so much hope, but the careful idea that life itself was beautiful because of our strife. We came to recognize that what we might have discovered to be an existentialism of the soul, that to exist as something conscious and alert and in tune with the world around was to exist in a degree of despair, but it is in this despair that we found our footing in a sense and a keen appreciation for that which reflected good things in life. For every discussion of the foibles of relationship drama we discussed the depths of how rewarding intimacy and emotional authenticity were for us. How love and all that was good in the world somehow outshone the darkness even though there was a sense that the dark was always there. There was a mutual understanding of our place in the universe, and he is one of the few souls who showed me truly that I was grounded in one way or another to the world around me, even if my head was somehow dissociated out into the voids of the unknown.

We took a trip once to Sombrio Beach on Vancouver Island for an overnight camping trip to recapture the feeling of our Outdoor Education experiences in primary school. On the shore of that beach and around our campfire we did truly experience that which had bonded us together all those years ago. Over countless cigarettes tossed into the embers of the fire, he and I found ourselves lying in different positions reading and annotating our respective books for the trip. I had brought Kierkegaard's Sickness unto Death and he a volume of Heidegger. While the waves lapped at the pebbles of the beach we traded out loud renditions of the passages we read. I would expound on Kierkegaard's mesmerizing account of the nature of self and despair and he would respond with equally meaningful analysis of his Heidegger. These are the memories encapsulative of my living experience with Will. A tradeoff of ideas tangentially related, relegated to one another in our own colloquial stylings. His blunt and authoritative with a mischievous deviance to his presentation, mine in a drawl monotone concealing my profound wonder at the words between us.

There were nights too where he would call or text me to say 'let me run this by you' and submit for my insight some element of his philosophical take on contemporary social issues. His responses would always hold with them a sharply humorous critique of my phrasing, often reminding me that I sometimes sound 'pretentious as fuck'. I carry that honorably to this day and in his memory, I shall for the remainder of my time here. He was one of the few people in my social sphere whom I could call in a manic bout of writing and pass the phrase or concept on to him that I was inventing who would look at what I said with a no-nonsense approach. Staunchly questioning me until I could formulate a thought that satisfied his need to know what the hell I was talking about. It was from these conversations that I came to be able to conceptualize my work better, and explain truly what I was working on. I owe a great deal of clarity in my theoretical work to his unique ability to combat what I was saying abrasively, but from a place of love and intellectual comradeship. Our relationship truly was one I count among the most important of my life.

An activity we undertook last summer was watching old films that had a similar thematic core to them: the darkness we all face in life. We viewed two films in this era: Easy Rider and Apocalypse Now. In both instances, upon the films conclusion and in many times throughout we would pause the film and steal away to my porch for a cigarette and a chat about the ideas therein. We would examine the fragile existentialism of being human. Of treading the razor's edge between darkness and enlightenment. There was a sense of that in him. Of being the snail on the edge of the razor blade that Marlon Brando monologues about in Apocalypse Now. Of being so close to the madness that he was seeing the true world beyond. I have felt myself there as well, but not so much in the way that he was. He was a timeless soul that stood as a testament to the extremes a human being can experience in a short but eventful life. He exemplified the spirit of these investigations into the human soul. That be it the open road or the snaking river of death, there is always something there to be learned, to be pondered, to know with respect to the fundamental nature of the spirit. I did not think in those moments that they were terrifically profound, but not all together mundane either. It was on the surface two people nearing 30 watching movies on the sofa over Domino's Pizza. But to me now in hindsight, there were many an instance of treasured profundity among those moments. As we pondered the descent of Captain Willard into the darkness, or the freedom and tragedy of life as Dennis Hopper and Peter Fonda are whisked into the great beyond along the Louisiana roadside, I now realize that these are those spontaneous reflections that come along at only the most opportune moments in life for us to expound upon.

I now sit in my memory of him as the emotional waves of his passing begin to gather upon the shore and think back upon these moments with great fondness. This was what he brought into my life. Not a sense of safe mundanity but a chance and a window from which I may explore the edges of that which is possible for the human spirit.

It is this spark of introspection I feel may be one of Will's most treasured contributions to the world he inhabited for such a short time. The ability to help those around him to see not only themselves more clearly, but to understand the nature of things beyond our scope of control or influence. To gain perspective in our liminality of life and mortality. He never said these things directly to me, but in reflecting now as I must, they were there in quite evident forms.

Following our summer of Dennis Hopper films, something quite lovely happened in Will's life that far outshines that darkness we had so often occupied together. Will met someone. I remember speaking with him the night before his first date with her and he had expressed that this felt different than any first date had before. He had talked to me often about the relationships of his past and in these talks we both expounded yet again on the pitfalls of the state of being in love as a social being. This is a topic my area of operational work has taken me and I had often meditated on the darkest aspects of love and being in relationships, but I noticed immediately in the onset of this talk that the air between us was different. On the lonely smoking bench nestled in the trees on campus, Will told me with unconfined excitement the initial joy he had of meeting her, and how deeply excited he was to have their first date.

I noticed within him a joyful exuberance that was almost childlike in its presentation-pure joy unencumbered by the weight of adulthood and past traumas. I could tell in that instance that she was someone he was deeply taken with but I never expected the blossoming of love and support and mutual solidarity that would emerge between them over the coming months. Although I only ever heard of their relationship through him, I cannot remember a single instance where his love for her, his joy for his partnership with her and his hope for the future was not staggeringly evident. He had truly in this pairing found true love. Not very long after they began dating he confided in me in his own way: *"Dude, I'm going to fucking marry this woman."* He was truly in his last months finding the happiness he so desperately deserved in this world. It seemed to me that in his partnership he was experiencing all those romanticized elements that lend to the ideal relationship. He found a soulmate. Someone who was by his own admission brilliantly inspiring professionally, personally, and romantically. He found that rare person in the world meant for him. Someone who he could not only be honest to about his imperfections, insecurities and demons, but someone who would listen with empathy and respond with loving care. To draw on the cliché, they were quite clearly meant for one another.

There were many a late night or early evening chats where Will expressed to me how lucky he felt to have found her. How she provided for him a concrete grounding for a future of happiness and fulfillment that he didn't always believe was possible for him or humans in general. It was beautiful to experience even tangentially as I did. I could see the lightness in his eyes and in his overall demeanor. He was changed for the better through his time with her and as a friend who had known him as a kid and in some of the darkest moments of his life, I was so happy for him to have found this light in his world. He would talk to me about magical moments on Salt Spring Island, intellectually and emotionally enriching dinners downtown and in every one of these chats he exuded such a pride for her. Not a pride that he had found her, but a pride that this person was so incredibly amazingly perfect for him.

He talked to me about his plans to marry her, to have a family, to settle down. To have that kind of life of love and family that he also so rightly deserved. I was beyond happy for my friend. I was proud of him too. Will was one of the most self-aware human beings I have ever known. Someone who could accurately psychoanalyze his mistakes in real time and provide to me and to himself realistically sound strategies to not only remedy them, but to be inherently better. He had his share of crises as we all do, and what I will offer is that even in these moments of absolute despair, he ended every meeting we shared with a hug, with what I have since attributed to him as his catchphrase to me: "much love brother, always."

***

And so we arrive at his passing. To say that I am shocked would be a grand understatement. To say that I am gutted, crushed, any other adjective would only approach a fraction of the despair and loss I now feel. As I sit to write this piece I have done so over the entire evening without sleeping. I have alternated between my writing desk, my sofa, and the bench outside of my house. I had wrapped myself in the shadows of the night to try as best as I may to understand the depths of the monumental permanence of this loss to my life and to those of us who also had the joy to know and to love Will. For hours after I hung up with his fiancée, I could myself not wrap my head around the gravity of his passing. It felt, for those initial hours as some temporary thing. Some momentary space in time where we wouldn't talk for a while. As if he were going on a trip and not taking his phone. The reality of the situation set in very hard around three in the morning last night and it is a heaviness I've still not fully grasped. I've since found solace in this piece of writing. In some symbolic means of holding on and perpetuating the immortality of our interactions into some preserved state.

I learned from her that I was the last person to speak to Will prior to his passing. I was experiencing my own crisis in my own life and I texted him randomly around 10:30pm. We chatted for a while about his recent bout of illness from the meal he had eaten, and the stay in Royal Jubilee. We joked even in these crucial moments about his weathered appearance. He said "I look like shit man" and I jokingly replied with 'going for that distressed Harry Dean Stanton look eh?" In reference to a film I had recently showed in my Death and Dying course only a few weeks ago. As we continued chatting he sent me a message that always precipitated a good interaction: "can I call you on the phone?" I responded that I would take just a moment and that I welcomed such an excuse to escape my prison in my home that was causing me such distress. I trekked again to that fabled bench outside my house. Struck the first Du Maurier Signature of the chat and said 'call whenever you're ready'. That was at 11:09pm.

We talked for nearly half an hour. First about my situation. He listened with empathy as he had always done, and then provided his bluntly loving takes on actions I should take. He did so from a place of validating my pain, of seeing my agency and humanity in this moment and from his empathetic space said to me that not only did I not deserve the abuse I was facing, but that I was too good of a person to be constantly be pressed down as I had been. He told me he was proud of me for making the decisions I did to stand up for myself and break the cycles that were hurting me. We shifted the conversation to how he was doing and recapped again his illness. We did so in a light hearted way, reflecting on both how I was glad he was feeling better and recovering, and also on how it was a sign of a true survivor that he was taking all these punches and still standing. In hindsight I am reminded of a line from The Boxer by Simon and Garfunkel: *"In the clearing stands a boxer, and a fighter by his trade, and he carries the reminders of every glove that laid him down, and cut him 'til he cried out, in his anger and his shame "I am leaving, I am leaving" But the fighter still remains."*

As the minutes ticked by, Will began to yawn and sound drowsy as he often did in our late night chats. He went to bed at normal hours unlike me and so this was late for him. He said he hadn't had enough sleep over the course of his illnesses and needed it badly. He asked if I'd be up for a while as he had only planned to sleep for a few hours then call me back. Not for his needs, but to check on me. One of the very final decisions he had made was to sacrifice sleep to make sure I was doing ok in my crisis. This endearing act is one that encapsulates his spirit. Baring his soul to the world, but also bending over backwards to help the people he loved in his life. I told him that he needed sleep but to call or text and if I was awake, I'd answer. We finalized our plans to have a goodbye hangout on Friday as I'd be moving away soon. He and I both said we were looking forward to it.

As the call dwindled Will's last words to me and perhaps to anyone were these, and they shall ring in my ears for the rest of my life:

"I love you so much man, have a goodnight, much love brother, see you Friday."

I haven't much else to add to this reflection other than a final lyric, a philosophical meditation by Brian Wilson, a lyric he and I had listened to on more than one occasion to which he had always had the same reaction: "Fuuck Man!"

I keep lookin' for a place to fit in
Where I can speak my mind
And I've been tryin' hard to find the people
That I won't leave behind
They say I got brains, but they ain't doin' me no good
I wish they could
Each time things start to happen again
I think I got somethin' good goin' for myself
But what goes wrong?
Sometimes I feel very sad
I guess I just wasn't made for these times

I will miss you very, very dearly my friend. I shall continue on in the murky greyness between light and dark in your name. I shall continue to forge the path of investigation into the human condition doing so feeling your words, your love, your wisdom guiding my words on the page. Our time was short, but it was rich in its meaning. I shall see you again someday, in the Great Gig in the Sky and so on. Thank you for the courage to approach the edge, to meditate on that which is darkest and most horrible. Thank you for your anchoring in this turgid world. Thanks for the memories, they shall infinitely live on through those you knew.

With the utmost love, goodbye.

TF

William G. Cockrell, Author

www.ingramcontent.com/pod-product-compliance
Lightning Source LLC
Chambersburg PA
CBHW032116040426
42449CB00007B/1247